AERO SERIES VOL. 26

MW01166331

GENERAL DYNAMICS F-16

WILLIAM G. HOLDER

and

WILLIAM D. SIURU, JR., PhD

ISBN 0-8168-0596-2

AERO PUBLISHERS, INC.
329 West Aviation Road, Fallbrook, CA 92028

Library of Congress Cataloging in Publication Data

Holder, William G   1937-
   General Dynamics F-16.

   (Aero series ; v. 26)
   Includes index.
   1. F-16 (Fighter planes)   I. Siuru, William D.,
joint
author. II. Title.
UG1242.F5H64   358.4'3   75-25245
ISBN 0-8168-0596-2

DEDICATION

To Andrea and Kathy

ACKNOWLEDGEMENTS

1. Air Force Systems Command Office of Information
2. Information Office, Air Force Flight Test Center, especially Captain Donald Brownlee
3. F-16 Joint Test Force, Air Force Flight Test Center, especially Major Robert Ettinger
4. Aeronautical Systems Division Office of Information, especially Major David Shea
5. General Dynamics Corporation
6. Ling-Temco-Vought Aerospace Corporation
7. Air Force Museum
8. Northrop Corporation
9. Rockwell International
10. U. S. Navy
11. McDonnell Douglas Corporation
12. Pratt & Whitney Aircraft
13. Dassault-Breguet of France
14. SAAB-SCANIA of Sweden

Special thanks are given to Wilbur Andrepont and Roger Talley for their photographic contributions and to Frank Stallman for graphic presentations.

TABLE OF CONTENTS

Chapter 1   The Birth of the Lightweight Fighter   . . .   7

Chapter 2   The F-16 Specifications   21

Chapter 3   The Flyoff   57

Chapter 4   The Other Faces of the F-16   81

Chapter 5   What It All Means   101

BIOGRAPHIES

Mr. Holder and Dr. Siuru are aerospace engineers who have been involved with the USAF's space and missile program for many years. Bill Holder has been at Wright-Patterson AFB, Ohio, the home of Air Force aviation technology, while Bill Siuru has had assignments as a career USAF officer at several organizations within the Air Force's Research and Development community. Both have written many articles and books about the space program, new and historic aircraft, and about other items of technology that are of interest to the public.

The F-16 Prototype

(USAF Photo)

Chapter I
The Birth of the Lightweight Fighter

From a fighter pilot's viewpoint, a fighter should be judged by its ability to outfly anything in the sky. Like the steeds of the knights of old, the fighter must be an extension of the man, responding instantaneously to his every demand. It must be agile and maneuverable; it must be dependable. The top fighters of the two world wars had these qualities. Planes such as the Sopwith Camel and the Spad, and like the Spitfire and the Mustang, could get into a dogfight, shooting an opponent out of the sky or flying him into the ground. With equal ease they could sneak up on a convoy of bombers or trucks, cause havoc, and depart as quickly as they had arrived. This is the story of the Air Force's newest air combat fighter, the F-16—a fighter pilot's fighter!

The easiest way to make a fighter more agile is to make it lighter. Then make it small, give it a gutsy engine that is economical so as to reduce the fuel load. Strip out all but the essential electronic gear. Over the years after World War II, fighter weights have increased just like the size and weight of the American automobile. More equipment was added to do more jobs and thus size had to be increased to get everything in. Then bigger engines and more fuel capacity had to be added to maintain maneuverability and range. Then more gear had to assist the pilot in handling the bigger craft with its more sophisticated equipment. On and on it went until late model fighters were heavier than some of the bombers of World War II.

The F-16 incorporates many new sophisticated devices. It is truly the aircraft of the 1980's.
(General Dynamics Photo)

Early in 1972, the United States Air Force took a determined step to correct the situation, the Lightweight Fighter Program was born. In Air Force jargon, the program is usually referred to by its initials, LWF. The Air Force had an added incentive for the LWF program. It is a well known fact around the aircraft business that aircraft costs can be directly correlated with aircraft weight. So all things being equal, usually a lighter plane means a cheaper one. With the cost of fighters like the F-15 Eagle going for about $15 million a copy, the Air Force knew that if they were to get a new combat fighter, it would have to be a significantly less expensive bird.

But before getting into the details of the F-16 and how it was developed and tested, let's spend a few moments looking at its ancestors.

Between the wars, the European countries showed more interest in lightweight fighters than the United States. Several lightweight concepts were developed like the wooden Caudron C.714 and the Bloch M. B. 700 that came out of France. The British developed the M.20 with its 12 gun arsenal.

As in many other areas, upon entering World War II, the United States had to play "catch-up ball" in the fighter arena. Impressed with enemy success with lightweight, agile fighters like the Japanese Zero and the Nazi Me 109, and coupled with the forecasted possibility of shortages of aircraft materials, the Air Corps started to get serious about a lightweight U.S. fighter. The requirements for a lightweight fighter given the Bell Aircraft Company in 1941 sounded like the specifications that would be written some thirty years later. The contract called for "a lightweight, inexpensive, highly maneuverable fighter."

What evolved on the designer's boards at Bell was a rather strange-looking bird carrying the title XP-77. The little fighter had a personality all its own with its squatty fuselage that looked nose heavy, its bubble canopy, and its tricycle landing gear. But America's first serious attempt at a lightweight fighter would never make it to the production lines. Problems during the development program caused the first flight to slip into 1944. By this time the wartime pace of aeronautical technology had passed her by. Advanced versions of such famous machines as the heavier P-47 and P-51 were in the thick of the fighting and were helping by no small measure to win the war. The war ended with no real U.S. lightweight fighter doctrine.

A lightweight fighter concept of sorts—the Sperry Messenger. The mounting shown carried the tiny plane aloft for an air-launch.
(USAF Photo)

8

A beautifully restored Spitfire shows its stuff at the 1975 Paris Air Show.   *(USAF Photo)*

The concept of carrying lightweight fighters aloft by balloon was attempted by the U. S. Navy. Shown is a Sparrowhawk being carried by the Navy Balloon "Macon."   *(U. S. Navy Photo)*

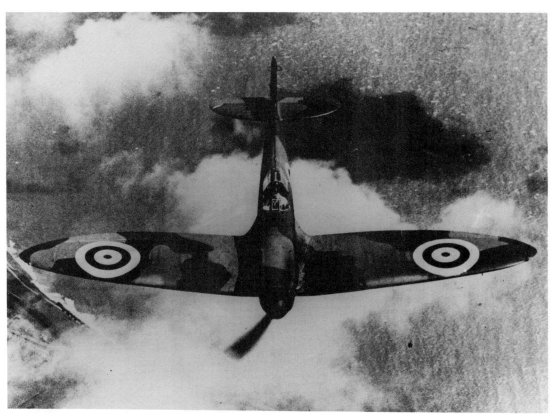

The nimble Spitfire showed the way in the Battle of Britain. (USAF Photo)

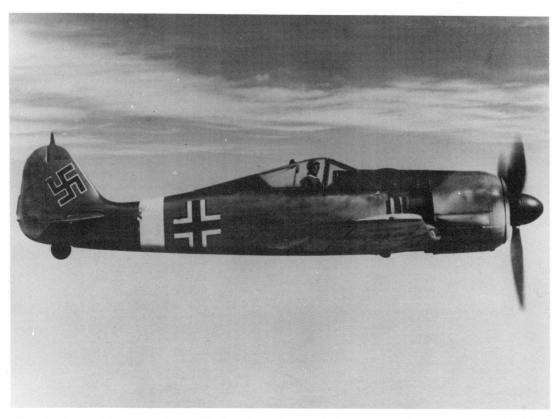

The nimble Nazi FW-190, along with the Me 109, provided a worthy adversary for allied fighters throughout the war. (AF Museum Photo)

The XP-77—Lightweight fighter, World War II style.

(USAF Photo)

Head-on view of the tiny XP-77 fighter.

(USAF Photo)

One of the real bulwark fighters of World War II—The P-47 Thunderbolt. This particular plane is a beautifully restored Thunderbolt belonging to the Confederate Air Force·

(Author Photo)

12

Compared to its P-47 running mate, the sleek P-51 Mustang was quite a lightweight herself.
(USAF Photo)

The XF-85 Goblin was a post-WW II attempt at a lightweight "parasite" fighter carried in the belly of a B-29 mother ship.
(USAF Photo)

Another "parasite fighter" concept using the B-36 mother ship and a modified F-84 Thunderjet.
(USAF Photo)

The F-111 Swingwing fighter continued the weight growth trend during the 1960's.   (USAF Photo)

THE GROWTH OF THE FIGHTER

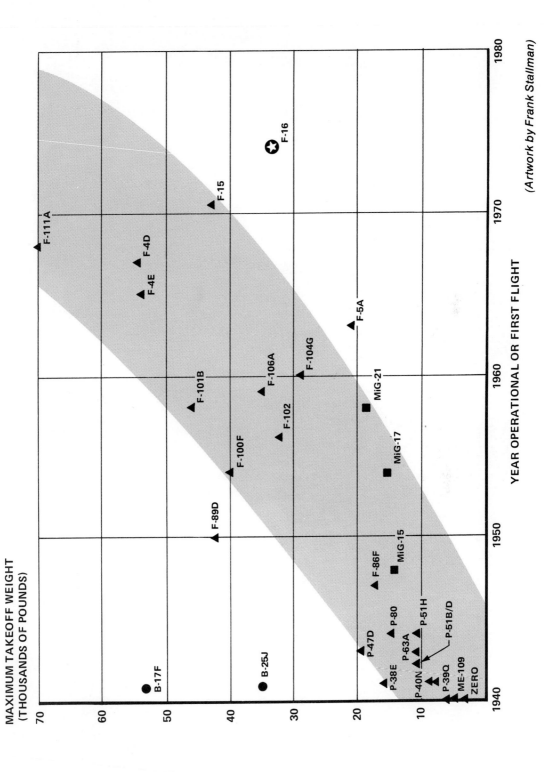

MAXIMUM TAKEOFF WEIGHT
(THOUSANDS OF POUNDS)

YEAR OPERATIONAL OR FIRST FLIGHT

(Artwork by Frank Stallman)

The F-106 built in the late 1950's was the last air superiority fighter built by General Dynamics. (USAF Photo)

The MiG-15 proved to be a nimble opponent for F-86 Sabre Jets during the Korean War.
(Photo by Robert Shenberger)

The Northrop F-5 fighter was the closest thing to a lightweight fighter during the I960's. The aircraft was never built in any numbers for the USAF. Many were built for foreign export.   *(USAF Photo)*

One of the latest versions of the F-5 series—the F-5F. (Northrop Corp.)

During the 1950's and 1960's, American fighters grew. Just look at the Century Series fighters and the brutish F-4 and the F-111. But during the same period some lessons were learned. The highly maneuverable, lightweight MiGs of the Korean, and later the Vietnam, wars proved again that the lightweight fighter was a viable concept. But it would not be until the 1970s that the United States would have a lightweight on its way into the inventory.

Like many other things, the term lightweight is only a relative term. Back in the 1940s, when the P-51 and P-47 weighed out for maximum takeoff at about five and ten tons respectively, the Zero and the Me 109, which each weighed less than three tons, were considered the small craft. In the 1950s and 1960s, the eight- to ten-ton MiGs were considerably smaller than their contemporaries. Today, the 33,000-pound F-16, at its maximum takeoff weight, is much smaller than the other more recent additions to the Air Force fighter inventory.

When the lightweight fighter program started in 1972, the idea was to have a two year development program and a one year test program. The intention was to demonstrate the advantages of the lightweight fighter and to prove several new design concepts. At the start of the program, the Air Force did not have the confidence in the concepts to allow it to go directly into production with them. The program was to produce "on-the-shelf hardware" that would let the Air Force develop a new fighter and to do so at a minimum technical risk. The

program was aimed at producing a prototype that would use various new concepts and show that they worked in practice.

The prototype approach is a new scheme the Department of Defense is using to procure new weapons. Rather than having to base the decision to go into production on paper studies and designs as has been done on most of the Air Force's more recent new aircraft, the idea is to build one or more prototypes (or for that matter any type of new weapon), test them extensively, and then decide whether or not to go into full-scale production. Like almost everything, the idea of prototyping is not something new; this is the way just about every aircraft was purchased by the Air Corps during the period between the world wars.

When the Air Force's Aeronautical Systems Division Prototype Programs Office at Wright-Patterson AFB, Ohio, asked for proposals to build prototype lightweight fighters, five aerospace companies responded with their ideas—General Dynamics, Boeing, Lockheed, LTV Aerospace, and Northrop. The experts looked over the proposals in great detail for several months and finally it was announced that General Dynamics and Northrop had won the competition. Each would build two prototypes and the two designs would be entered into a fly-off to determine which the Air Force would put into production. General Dynamics would build their proposed single engined F-16, while Northrop would construct the dual-engined F-17. The lightweight fighter was becoming a reality!

Chapter II
The F-16 Specifications

The F-16 packs a lot of punch in a small package and thus has earned the title "a fighter pilot's fighter." It has twice the maneuver capability of current U. S. fighters and this capability is combined with twice the combat radius when operating in the air superiority role; that is, in air-to-air combat. On air-to-ground missions it has half again the combat radius of our current fighters carrying heavy bomb loads, a visual weapon delivery accuracy equal to the latest attack aircraft, and a much superior self-defense capability.

The F-16 is 47 feet 2 inches long, with a wingspan of 31 feet 10 inches including two wing-tip mounted missiles. From the ground to the tip of the vertical tail, the craft measures 16 feet 4 inches. The F-16 has a design gross weight of 21,500 pounds with a maximum operating weight tipping the scales at 33,000. The craft can carry an amazing 6,600 pounds of fuel within the internal structure of the aircraft. On the various external mounts on the F-16, 15,000 pounds of payload can be accommodated. This provides ample capacity for bombs, missiles, and auxiliary fuel tanks. Because it is small, it makes a poor target. It will be difficult to detect either visually or by radar, and even if it is detected, it will be hard to hit.

The F-16 is powered by the Pratt and Whitney F100-PW-100 afterburning turbofan engine. This is basically the same engine that is already used in the Air Force's newest fighter in production, the F-15 Eagle. By using the same engine as that in the Eagle, the Air Force will save a tremendous amount of money. First, a new engine will not have to be developed and tested, which is a very costly process. The F100 is proven and in full production now. Secondly, this engine commonality will result in several millions of dollars saving in training of maintenance personnel, in the cost of specialized maintenance tools, and in the number of spare parts that have to be kept in the supply inventory.

Even though the F100 is called an advanced technology engine, it was a mature engine before it made its first flight in the F-16. By October of 1973, it had successfully completed its 150 hour endurance test, the most severe test in aviation history. In this test it operated under conditions that simulated over thirty hours of flight at a speed of 1,500 miles per hour and another 38 hours at conditions that simulated flight at 1,100 miles per hour.

The F-16 rolls in after a 1975 air show performance at Wright-Patterson Air Force Base.

(Talley Photo)

INTERIOR ARRANGEMENT

Cross sections ...

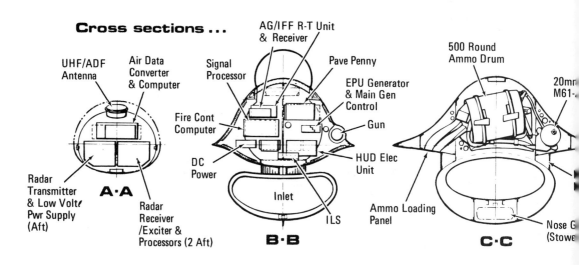

A·A

UHF/ADF Antenna

Air Data Converter & Computer

Radar Transmitter & Low Volt Pwr Supply (Aft)

Radar Receiver /Exciter & Processors (2 Aft)

B·B

AG/IFF R-T Unit & Receiver

Signal Processor

Pave Penny

Fire Cont Computer

EPU Generator & Main Gen Control

Gun

DC Power

HUD Elec Unit

Inlet

ILS

C·C

500 Round Ammo Drum

20mm M61-

Ammo Loading Panel

Nose G (Stowe

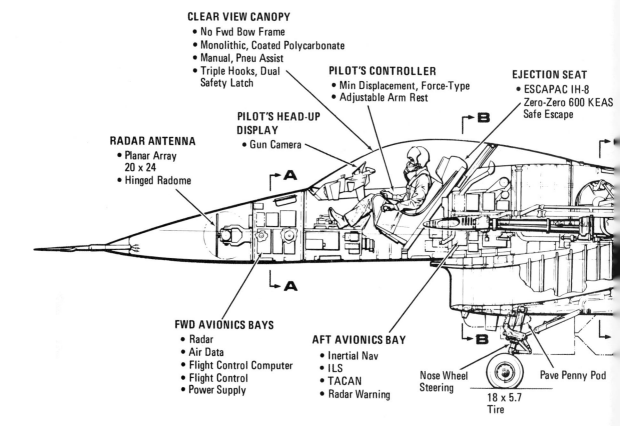

CLEAR VIEW CANOPY
- No Fwd Bow Frame
- Monolithic, Coated Polycarbonate
- Manual, Pneu Assist
- Triple Hooks, Dual Safety Latch

PILOT'S CONTROLLER
- Min Displacement, Force-Type
- Adjustable Arm Rest

EJECTION SEAT
- ESCAPAC IH-8 Zero-Zero 600 KEAS Safe Escape

PILOT'S HEAD-UP DISPLAY
- Gun Camera

RADAR ANTENNA
- Planar Array 20 x 24
- Hinged Radome

FWD AVIONICS BAYS
- Radar
- Air Data
- Flight Control Computer
- Flight Control
- Power Supply

AFT AVIONICS BAY
- Inertial Nav
- ILS
- TACAN
- Radar Warning

Nose Wheel Steering

18 x 5.7 Tire

Pave Penny Pod

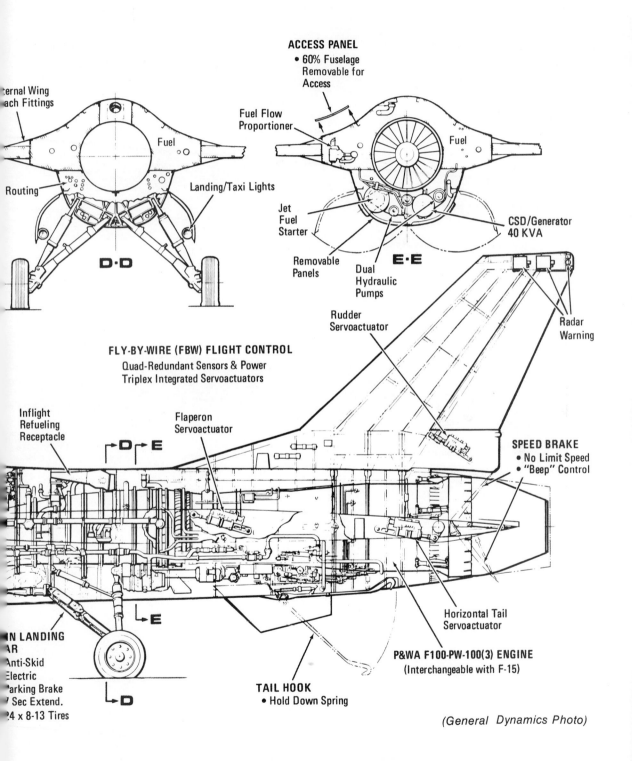

ACCESS PANEL
- 60% Fuselage Removable for Access

ternal Wing ach Fittings

Fuel Flow Proportioner

Fuel

Fuel

Routing

Landing/Taxi Lights

Jet Fuel Starter

CSD/Generator 40 KVA

D·D

E·E

Removable Panels

Dual Hydraulic Pumps

Rudder Servoactuator

Radar Warning

FLY-BY-WIRE (FBW) FLIGHT CONTROL
Quad-Redundant Sensors & Power
Triplex Integrated Servoactuators

Inflight Refueling Receptacle

Flaperon Servoactuator

D **E**

SPEED BRAKE
- No Limit Speed
- "Beep" Control

E

N LANDING ·AR
·nti-Skid
·lectric
·arking Brake
· Sec Extend.
·4 x 8-13 Tires

D

Horizontal Tail Servoactuator

TAIL HOOK
- Hold Down Spring

P&WA F100-PW-100(3) ENGINE
(Interchangeable with F-15)

(General Dynamics Photo)

23

DESIGNED FOR

Ω HIGH PERFORMANCE/MANEUVERABILITY

👤   PILOT EFFECTIVENESS

❚   WEAPON DELIVERY

\#   LIGHT WEIGHT

S LOW COST

∞∞   RELIABILITY/MAINTAINABILITY/ SUPPORTABILITY

∞   FLEXIBILITY/GROWTH

👤❚ *Simplified, integrated stores management system with versatile pilot control of selected air-to-air and air-to-ground weapons and displays using controls on the throttle grip and flight controller – "eyes on target"*

👤❚ *Head-up multimode display and fire control computer allows the pilot to select various gunnery-, missile- and bombing-mode displays and energy-maneuverability data – "eyes on target"*

👤❚ *Radar/EO display for multiple air-to-air target display and Maverick/Hobo video display*

👤❚ *20 to 25 n.mi., coherent radar; all-angle search, and range track*

∞∞ Ω *Triple redundant air data sources for the flight control system including nose and fuselage probes and angle-of-attack cones*

∞∞ ❚ *Forward avionics bay containing all radar line replaceable units and other equipment – easy maintenance*

∞ *Dedicated avionics provisions and growth space*

👤❚ Ω *High-g cockpit with 30° seat and raised heel rest; side stick pilot's flight controller for precise control inputs during combat maneuvers – 17% tracking improvement at high-g*

∞∞ Ω \# *Quadrex electronics and electrical power supply for the flight control system – two-fail-operate*

Ω \# S *Inlet mounted beneath the fuselage to minimize airflow disturbances during aircraft maneuvers; also eliminates gun-gas ingestion, and with inlet forward of the nose wheel, minimizes risk of FOD*

∞ *10% oversized air-inlet duct to accommodate engine thrust growth*

👤❚ *High-visibility bubble canopy wi[th] forward bow frame, 360-degre[e] around vision, 40-degree down the-side vision and 15-degree [?] over-the-nose vision*

FS253[?]

Ω *Forebody strakes provide effec[t] vortex control – increased lift, [?] directional stability*

Ω \# *Wing-body blending for aerodyna[mic] structural, and volume benefits*

THE F-16A AIR COMBAT FIGHTER

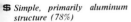 • SMALL • LIGHT WEIGHT • SIMPLE

HIGH PERFORMANCE AT LOW COST

$ Simple, primarily aluminum structure (78%)

$ 11% additional structural design margin

$ Modular construction

Ω Selective use of graphite composites — tails, speed brakes, landing gear doors, lower fuselage doors

Ω Flying boom air refueling receptacle

⌁ 20mm M61 gun with 515 rounds and two to six AIM-9 sidewinder missiles

∞ $ Standardization and multiple useage of parts; high useage of off-the-shelf components

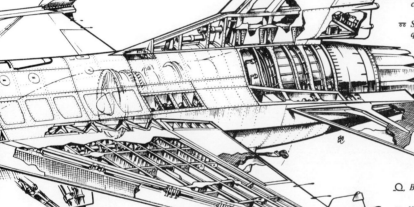

Ω Single vertical tail yields better directional stability at combat angles of attack

Ω # $ Single engine — used on the F-15 aircraft

∞ Single-rail engine removal and engine quick disconnects

Ω Barrier arrestment tail hook

∞ Hinged doors and panels for rapid access to all equipment

$ Integrated servoactuators on the primary flight control surfaces

Ω Twin clam-shell type speed brakes each side of the engine nozzle inboard of the horizontal tails

⌁ 9 external store stations carry 10,000 pounds with full internal fuel; freefall and electro-optical (EO) guided bombs and dispensers and air-to-ground missiles; other weapons, ECM pods, and fuel tanks

Ω ∞ Wing planform and thickness optimized for "combat arena of the future"

Ω Automatic leading-edge maneuver flaps maintain effective lift coefficients at high angles of attack

Ω # $ Relaxed longitudinal static stability/ fly-by-wire flight control system improves control and performance

(General Dynamics Photo)

Details of the intake and forward fuselage are clearly visible in this photograph. *(Talley Photo)*

The markings shown on the F-16's intake cowling are not aircraft shot down but show the number of airshows where the little bird has thrilled crowds. *(Talley Photo)*

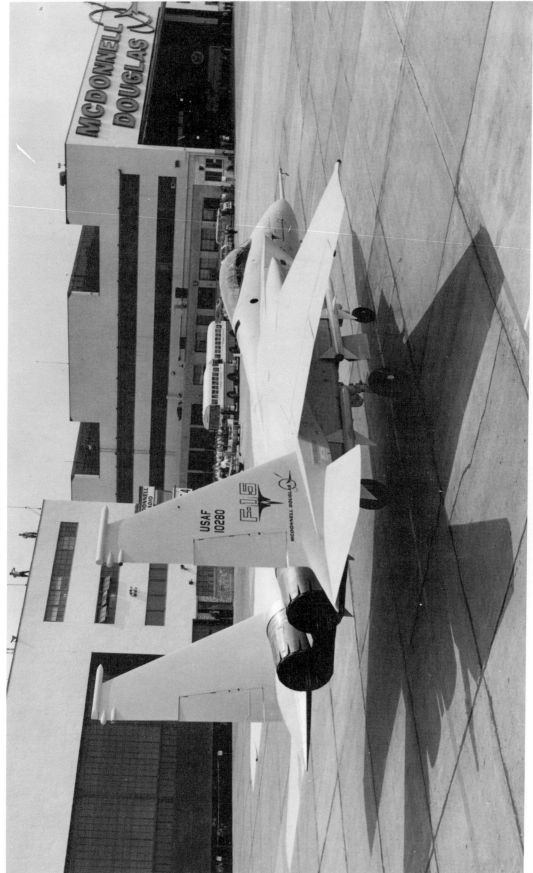

The F-16's powerplant, the F100 engine; a pair is used in the F-15 Eagle. (McDonnell-Douglas Photo)

F-16 GENERAL ARRANGEMENT

DATA

Wing Area . . . . 280 Sq Ft
Aspect Ratio 3.0
L.E. Sweep 40⁰

WEIGHTS

Design T.O.G.W. . . . . 21,500 lb
Max T.O.G.W. . . . . 33,000 lb
Max Ext Load Capacity . . . . 15,200 lb

ENGINE

Pratt & Whitney F100-PW-100(3)

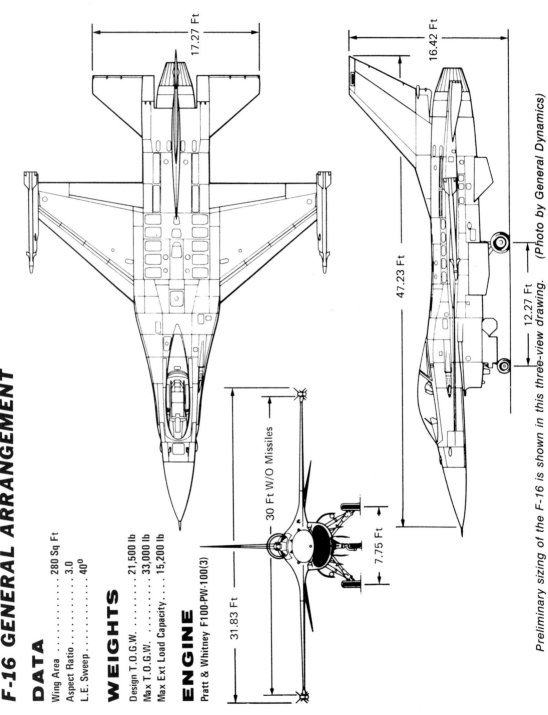

17.27 Ft

16.42 Ft

47.23 Ft

12.27 Ft

30 Ft W/O Missiles

7.75 Ft

31.83 Ft

Preliminary sizing of the F-16 is shown in this three-view drawing.   *(Photo by General Dynamics)*

development maturity.....

F100 qualification succesfully demonstrated engine durability at sustained maximum power and high Mach number conditions equivalent to over 3000 air superiority missions.

ENGINE TEST HOURS

28,000
24,000
20,000
16,000
12,000
8,000
4,000
0

F-15 OPERATIONAL INTRODUCTION

YF-16 FIRST FLIGHT

QT

F-15 FIRST FLIGHT

PFRT

1970
1971
1972
1973
1974

History of the highly successful F100 engine.

(Pratt & Whitney Photo)

The Pratt and Whitney engine is an axial flow, low bypass, high compression ratio, twin spool engine with an annular combustion chamber and is equipped with an afterburner. Its ten-stage compressor is driven by a two-stage turbine, while the three-stage turbofan is driven by two additional stages of the turbine. The engine is 191 inches long, weighs 3,020 pounds, and is 36 inches in diameter at the engine inlet.

Advanced technology is found in just about every portion of the engine. The advanced components coupled with extensive use of improved materials make the engine lighter and allow it to produce more thrust. It produces over eight pounds of thrust for every pound of engine weight, and represents a major improvement over previous engines. The engine is designed to produce essentially no exhaust smoke thus making it difficult to detect by the enemy.

The engine is made up of five major modules: the fan, the core consisting of the compressor, combuster and compressor-drive turbine, the turbine to drive the fan, the afterburner and exhaust nozzle, and the gearbox. Each module is completely interchangeable from engine to engine. This means an entire engine is not idle when repairs have to be made on one of the modules. The ailing module is simply pulled out and replaced with a spare and the craft is on its way again. This significantly reduces aircraft down-time and the number of engine spares that must be kept on hand. This modular concept has already proved itself on the F-15 program where during the flight test program ninety-five percent of the engine repairs were done on the modules rather than the complete engines.

The remainder of the F-16 incorporates a number of advanced technologies and design innovations that have not been previously combined into a single aircraft. But this is to be expected since the original purpose of the lightweight fighter program was to gather advanced concepts and technologies and put them together into a prototype, and prove them by putting the prototype through a rigorous flight test program. In fact, no other fighter makes such extensive use of advanced technology and there is different philosophy employed in the use of these advances. In the past, using advanced technology usually meant an increase in aircraft cost and complexity. In the F-16 it is different! The technologies were selected and integrated in such a manner that they decreased the overall weight of the craft by

Decals from flying outfits all over the world adorn the F-16 engine cover of the Paris Air Show F-16.
(Photo by Roger Talley)

(Pratt & Whitney Photo)

Check-out of an F100 engine.

PRATT & WHITNEY AIRCRAFT

F100-PW-100 AUGMENTED TURBOFAN ENGINE

FACT SHEET

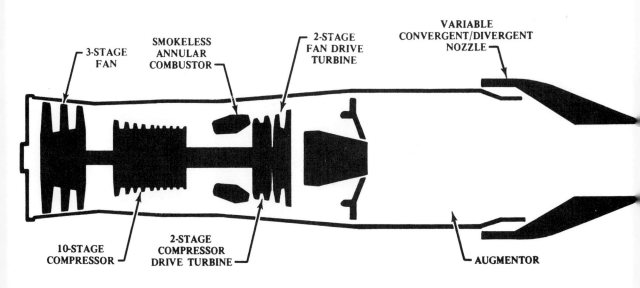

CHARACTERISTICS:

MAXIMUM THRUST (FULL AUGMENTATION)	25,000-POUND (111.2 kN) CLA
INTERMEDIATE THRUST (NON-AUGMENTED)	15,000-POUND (66.7 kN) CLAS
WEIGHT	3020 POUNDS (1371 kg)
LENGTH	191 INCHES (4.85 m)
INLET DIAMETER	36 INCHES (0.91 m)
MAXIMUM DIAMETER	46.5 INCHES (1.18 m)
BYPASS RATIO	0.6
OVERALL PRESSURE RATIO	24 to 1

HISTORY:

DESIGN BEGAN	AUGUST 1968
DEVELOPMENT CONTRACT AWARD	MARCH 1970
PRELIMINARY FLIGHT RATING TEST (PFRT) COMPLETED	FEBRUARY 1972
FIRST FLIGHT	JULY 1972
QUALIFICATION TEST (QT) COMPLETED	OCTOBER 1973
FLIGHT TIME (THROUGH JANUARY 1975)	8,500 HOURS
TOTAL DEVELOPMENT TEST TIME (THROUGH JANUARY 1975)	32,000 HOURS
OPERATIONAL INTRODUCTION (LUKE AIR FORCE BASE)	NOVEMBER 1974

(Pratt & Whitney Chart)

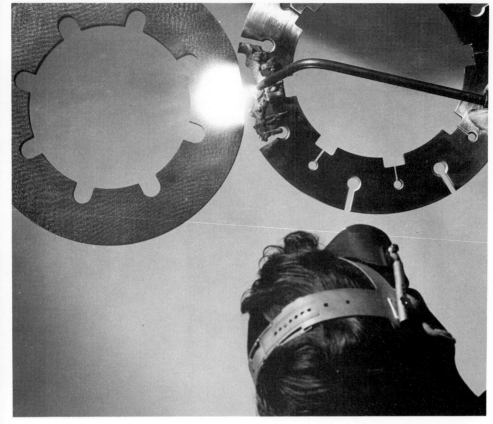

Test by Fire—A 3,000-degree acetylene flame had little effect on a Goodyear-developed carbon-composite aircraft brake disk (top), but a steel aircraft brake disk of the same relative size was severely burned and melted. Goodyear carbon disk brakes will be installed on the Air Force's F-16 fighter. (Goodyear Photo)

Rear portion of the F-16 prototype. (General Dynamics Photo)

Photo provides excellent detail of one of two Sidewinder missiles and its wingtip rail launcher.(General Dynamics Photo)

(General Dynamics Photo)

The F-16 carries the same Vulcan 20mm gun as the F-4E shown above.

(USAF Photo)

thousands of pounds and this led to a reduction in the costs of the aircraft and its development.

The F-16 is made lightweight without extensive use of exotic materials or making the craft weaker. The plane's structure is mostly aluminum, 78 percent, and four-fifths of this is made up of plain sheet aluminum. Titanium, special steel, and advanced composite materials make up less than some ten percent of the structure, and these were used only where these special materials were absolutely needed to do the job. As an example of the strength of the F-16, the plane is designed to be able to make up to 9 g maneuvers with full internal fuel tanks. In the past, fighters could only pull 7-1/3 g's with a 60 to 80 percent fuel load in their internal tanks.

As a further means of cost savings, identical and interchangeable horizontal tail surfaces, ventral fins and wing flap/ailerons are used for the left and right side of the airplane. Additionally, eighty percent of the main landing gear is interchangeable from the port to starboard sides.

Externally, the F-16 looks in many ways more like a lifting body spacecraft than a manned interceptor. The F-16's stubby wings, which join the fuselage far back from the nose, have a surface area of 300 square feet and have a forty-degree sweepback. The tail surfaces are basically the same shape, but have

a slight droop. This external appearance is the result of the blended wing-body concept adopted for the craft. This configuration provides lift from the aircraft body at high angles of attack, gives less wetted surface area, provides more internal fuel volume, and results in a more rigid structure. And this is all accomplished with reduced structural weight! The additional lift from the body is needed at high angles of attack, as in this attitude the lift contribution of the wings starts to fall off.

The pilot of the F-16 uses the "fly-by-wire" technique to control the craft's control surfaces. In this concept, the normal mechanical linkages, cables, and bell cranks are replaced by direct electrical commands transmitted by wire from the pilot's controls to the individual actuators that move the plane's control surfaces. The fly-by-wire technique offers better handling qualities, more precise and responsive control, which is especially important in combat situations, increased reliability and survivability, greater maneuverability, and a simplified aircraft structure with more room for the all-important fuel. There is no mechanical backup for the wire controlled systems, but there are four channels for the electric signals to make their way from the pilot's hands to the necessary actuator. Thus, the fly-by-wire method provides quadruple

In this photo the pilot appears to be cantilevered out into space. (Andrepont Photo)

redundancy.

Because of the high maneuver capability of the F-16, special considerations had to be given to the physical tolerance level that the pilot could withstand. Thus, the design includes a high-g cockpit. In this cockpit, the seatback angle is thirty degrees rather than the thirteen degrees normally found in fighter craft. By sitting in a more reclined position the pilot's tolerance to high g's is greatly increased. He can track targets better while under high g's, and his view to the rear is improved with this seat position.

In order to perform maneuvers with great precision, the F-16 pilot is provided with a side-stick controller with a built-in armrest. The F-16 is also equipped with a bubble canopy and windshield that allows the pilot a panoramic view of his surroundings. He can see 360 degrees in the horizontal direction, 40 degrees down over-the-side and 15 degrees over-the-nose. The canopy is made of polycarbonate, a new plastic material that is virtually indestructible. The high-g cockpit, the side-stick controller, and the clear view canopy and windshield are all features that will be truly appreciated by the pilot when he gets the F-16 in the thick of combat.

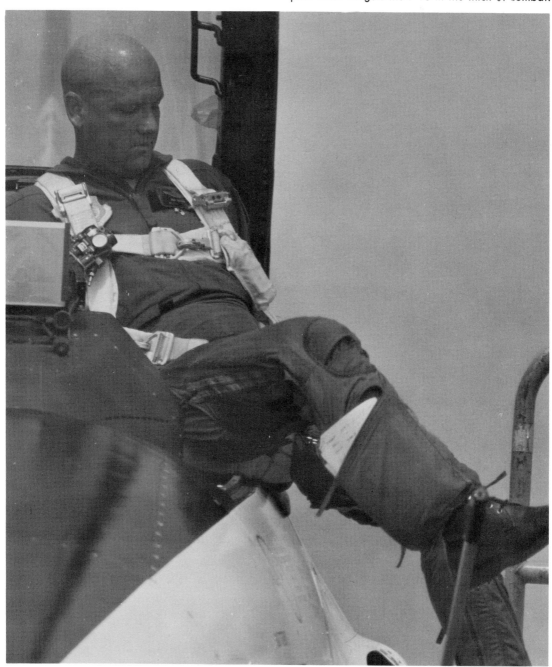

General Dynamics test pilot peels out of the F-16's compact cockpit after a flight performance.

(Talley Photo)

A low angle shot provides good detail of the F-16's low-mounted air intake.
(General Dynamics Photo)

This side view shows the pencil-thin forward fuselage of the F-16. (General Dynamics Photo)

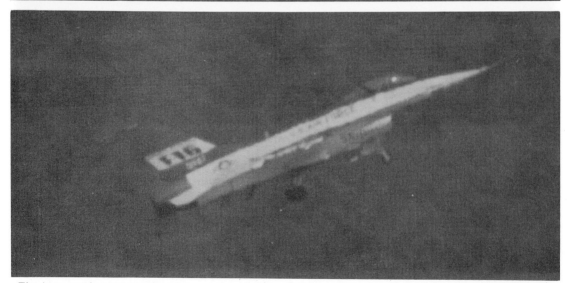

The long-angle camera provides a series of shots showing the F-16 and an F-4 both performing max-imum performance takeoffs. The F-16 is nearly out of sight by the time the F-4's gear has cleared the runway.
(Talley Photo)

(Photo by Wil Andrepont)

Ready to "Get it on!"

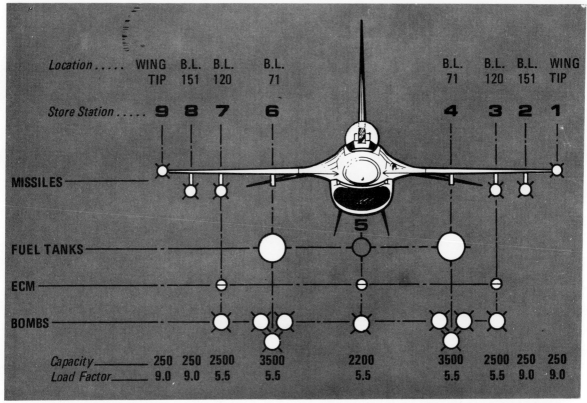

Location.....	WING TIP	B.L. 151	B.L. 120	B.L. 71		B.L. 71	B.L. 120	B.L. 151	WING TIP
Store Station.....	9	8	7	6	5	4	3	2	1
Capacity	250	250	2500	3500	2200	3500	2500	250	250
Load Factor	9.0	9.0	5.5	5.5	5.5	5.5	5.5	9.0	9.0

Location of stores on F-16. (General Dynamics Photo)

If an emergency arises that requires the pilot to ditch his craft, there is a triple redundant emergency egress system that will insure his safe departure from the plane. Normally when the pilot has to leave, first the canopy will be pivoted back and upwards, then the pilot will be ready to use the ejection seat. If for some reason the system fails, the canopy can be jettisoned by explosive bolts. If all else fails, the pilot will be able to unlatch the canopy manually and push it up into the airstream. The airstream will force the canopy open so that the pilot can get out.

Even though the F-16 is in the lightweight class, it still packs a big punch when it comes to armament, and the range and versatility in weapons it can carry. To begin with, in the fuselage just behind the pilot on the craft's left side is mounted an M61A1 Vulcan 20mm gun. This Gatling type gun has the capability to fire from 4000 to 6000 rounds per minute. On the wing tips and below the wings are pylons or hardpoints for carrying a wide range of weapons, or in military jargon, stores. For example, the Sidewinder missile can be fired from its location on the wing tips. A variety of different kinds of bombs, including the newest in laser-controlled types, can be dropped from the pylons below the wings or fuselage. Pods can also be attached below the wings or fuselage to carry electronic countermeasures to spoof the enemy. Finally, thousands of pounds of extra fuel can be carried in externally mounted wing tanks to give the F-16 even more range. With a full fuel load in the plane's internal tanks, the F-16 can carry approximately 11,500 pounds externally without exceeding the 33,000 pound maximum takeoff weight. By decreasing the internal fuel load somewhat, the externally carried load can be increased to 15,000 pounds. While carrying stores externally, the F-16 still can fly and maneuver at high g's, an important factor when the plane is used in the air superiority role.

Although lightweight, the craft has sufficient range to "get to the battle" with enough fuel left to "stay with the fight." It has 2.3 times the combat range of current U. S. fighters on an air-superiority mission provided each airplane carries the air-to-air weapons each was designed to carry, and each flies the same combat maneuvers. Its very high thrust-to-weight ratio and its aerodynamic design permit it to outfly any craft the enemy is known to have. In fact it has such good turning ability, it can practically run circles around its opponents. Not only does the craft give twice the combat radius, but when compared to other recent air superiority fighters, it does so at about half the weight and for less than one-half the cost. It has been projected that when the F-16 gets into the Air Force inventory, it will save over 100 million gallons of fuel every year. This is an important factor during today's energy crunch and with today's high jet fuel prices.

41

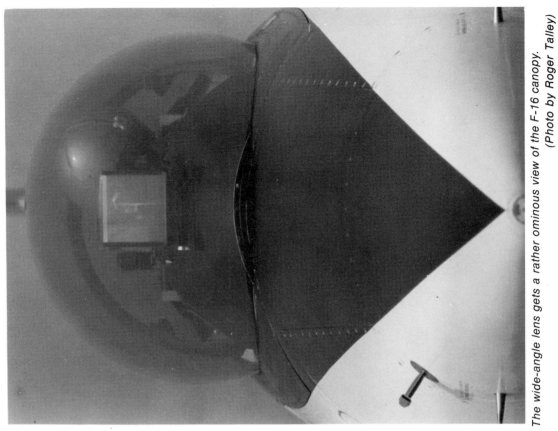

The wide-angle lens gets a rather ominous view of the F-16 canopy.
(Photo by Roger Talley)

Power cables in place, the F-16 gets ready to go. Note inboard bomb rack
carrying six conventional bombs. *(Photo by Wil Andrepont)*

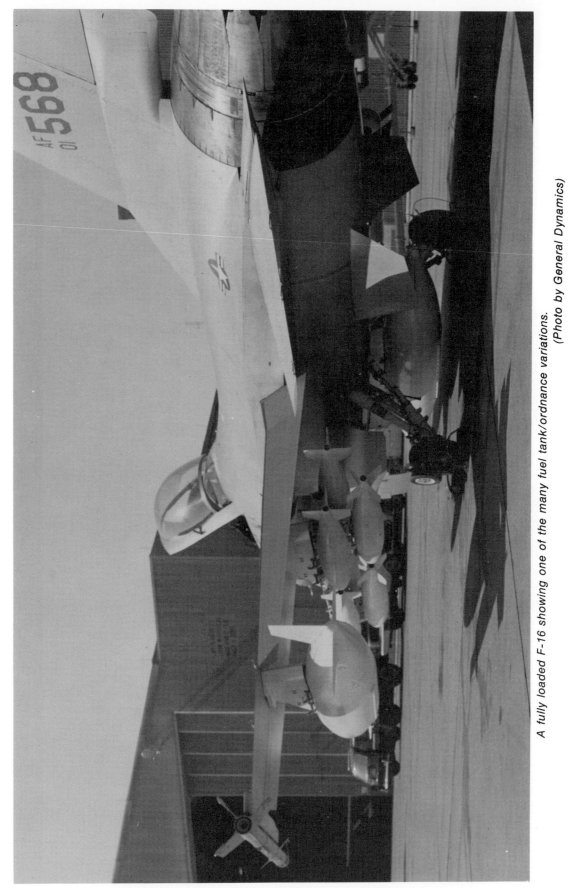

A fully loaded F-16 showing one of the many fuel tank/ordnance variations.
(Photo by General Dynamics)

Loaded with dummy ordnances, the F-16 prototype gets a tow.

(Photo by Andrepont)

What one might call a full load. *(Photo by General Dynamics)*

In a 1975 air show appearance at Wright-Patterson AFB, Ohio, the F-16 flies alongside an F-4 Phantom, which it later flew circles around. *(Photo by Roger Talley)*

A shot looking at the F-16's super-simple instrument panel.

(General Dynamics Photo)

The electronics, or avionics gear to be more precise, have been designed for both the F-16's air superiority and air-to-ground strike roles. The fire control system, including the radar, the display consoles, and the pilot's controls have been designed with an "eyes-out-of-the-cockpit" concept in mind. In other words, the pilot can fly his plane and get his weapons on target without having to look away from the outside to work his controls and read his gauges. The key fire control jobs are integrated to provide the pilot with quick-reaction, finger-tip control of the displays and weapons. Even when flying at high g's, the pilot can make his maneuvers without taking his eyes off the target, be it another airplane or a target on the ground. The fire control system has all-weather capability and can be used for both visual and blind delivery of the weapon. The radar is of the type that can look down and present informa-

tion to the pilot discriminating between the targets and the ground clutter. Besides the fire control apparatus, the craft carries the most modern of navigation equipment including a highly accurate inertial navigation system. Besides the normal radio communications gear, the craft has a backup voice communications set.

The avionics, and for that matter many of the other systems, incorporate advanced built-in self-test, fault isolation, and condition indicators. These items will reduce the time and manpower needed to find the problem and make the repairs. It has been estimated that the maintenance of the F-16 will require 60 percent fewer maintenance people than today's fighters.

The design of the F-16 is in tune with the times. It is built with economy in mind, but it does not sacrifice performance and reliability to get this economy.

There just isn't much equipment required to get the F-16 going. *(Photo by Roger Talley)*

YF-17 Lightweight Fighter—The advanced USAF/Northrop YF-17 Fighter prototype is a single-place, Mach 2 Class air superiority fighter designed around advanced aerodynamic features for exceptional maneuverability and stability during air-to-air combat. The prototype weighs approximately 21,000 pounds, takeoff weight, which includes the M-61 rapid firing cannon and ammunition and two heat-seeking missiles. The YF-17 is powered by two General Electric YJ101 turbojet engines, rated in the 15,000-pound thrust class. The wing span is 35 feet; length is 55.5 feet; height is 14.5 feet; and wing area is 350 square feet.   *(Northrop Photo)*

To many, the F-16 is the best-looking aircraft ever built.   (General Dynamics Photo)

F-16—the Pilot's fighter!   *(USAF Photo)*

A low angle shot provides a good detail of the F-16's low-mounted air intake.

(General Dynamics Photo)

One of the two prototypes takes to the air from Edwards AFB during the flyoff.
(General Dynamics Photo)

Loaded for bear! The VF-16 shows an impressive load being carried on both under-wing pylons.
(General Dynamics Photo)

The details of the F-16's main gear are clearly visible in this photo.   *(General Dynamics Photo)*

F-16 shown with ordnance on all four wing pylons and auxiliary fuel tank under fuselage. Grey color is now standard color for the aircraft.   *(General Dynamics Photo)*

The F-16 sporting its initial camouflage paint job. This colorful scheme would later be abandoned. (General Dynamics)

The F-16's super sleek lines are quite visible in this head-on photo. Note auxiliary fuel tanks on wing pylons.   *(General Dynamics Photo)*

The California landscape is spread out under the YF-16 in this shot.   *(USAF Photo)*

F-16 check-out operations (Photo by W. Siuru)

The F-16's extremely simple ground support equipment. (Photo by W. Siuru)

Neil Anderson, GD test pilot, after a flight in the F-16. (Photo by N. Siuru)

Thirty-degree tilted pilot's seat. (Photo by W. Siuru)

The Edwards AFB desert is a blur under the YF-16 as it really pours on the coal.
(General Dynamics Photo)

The two prototypes in flight. The blended fuselages are quite evident in this picture.
(General Dynamics Photo)

Chapter III
The Flyoff

Part of the Air Force's current prototyping philosophy is the fly-off. Here the competing craft are put through their paces being flown on missions that represent what they will see in actual operation, and probably even more. They are wrung out to see where their components might fail, if they have weaknesses in such areas as maneuverability, performance, or maintenance. They are judged as to which will do the job best. Finally, on the basis of this fly-off, coupled with information and studies from the craft's development program, the Air Force decides if the concept is ready for production and which of the contenders should be given the go-ahead to begin production.

The F-16 had some stiff competition from the other contender in the Lightweight Fighter Program, the F-17 built by Northrop. In recent years Northrop has had considerable success with the F-5 lightweight fighter it builds to supply the needs of air forces around the world. The USAF uses a two-seat version of the F-5 as a trainer and gives it the designation the T-38 Talon. For the past several years, Northrop has been working on a successor to the F-5 for service in the foreign air forces. The successor was the Northrop P-530 Cobra. Therefore, when the USAF asked for bids for the prototype for the lightweight fighter, Northrop was ready with a derivative of the Cobra, the P-600 or F-17.

The F-17 has two engines which, while dual engines add to weight, cost and complexity, do improve the flight safety. The two engines in the F-17 are the new YJ101-GE-100's developed by General Electric. This 15,000 pound thrust class engine is based on a scaled-down version of the gas-generator core of the F101-GE-100 turbofan used in the Rockwell B-1 supersonic bomber. This gives the F-17 a total of 30,000 pounds of thrust compared to a total of 25,000 pounds found in the F-16. The F-17 is slightly larger than its competitor, being 55½ feet long and having a wing span of 35 feet. It is 14½ feet to the top of its twin tails. The weights of the two craft are comparable as are their Mach 2 top speeds, which translates to 1320 miles-per-hour at 40,000 feet.

The YF-16 number one aircraft just completed and ready for paint.　　　*(General Dynamics Photo)*

The YF-17 carried Sidewinder missiles on its wingtips like its F-16 counterpart.   (Northrop Photo)

The sleek forward fuselage of the YF-17 is vividly illustrated by this photo.   (Northrop Photo)

During the prototype construction, the wing is lowered to mate with the fuselage.
Dynamics Photo)   *(General Dynamics Photo)*

On December 13, 1973, the red, white, and blue YF-16 was rolled out of the hangar at the General Dynamics plant in Forth Worth, Texas. This first F-16 was ready in less than two years after the start of the Lightweight Fighter Program. Then several weeks after roll-out, the prototype was dismantled enough so that it would fit through the nose door of a giant C-5 Galaxy transport. The F-16 was then flown in the cavernous interior of the C-5 to Edwards AFB to begin the flight test program for the flyoff.

It was not a great start, in fact the first flight of the F-16 was not even planned that 20th day of January 1974. But planned or not, the new fighter took to the air with General Dynamics engineering test pilot Philip F. Oestricher at the controls. It happened during what had been planned as a high-speed taxi test when the F-16 sustained minor damage to its right horizontal stabilizer. Phil Oestricher elected to take off in the F-16 rather than attempt to get the craft stopped. He flew the craft for six minutes without any problems and ended the flight by a routine and standard landing.

The first planned flight occurred a few days later on February 4, 1974, again with Oestricher at the controls. This time he got to fly the craft for 90 minutes. After a routine takeoff, he climbed to 15,-000 feet and then cycled the landing gear. Then with the gear up, he took the plane up to 30,000 feet at a speed of 300 knots. At this altitude, he performed pitch, roll, and yaw maneuvers and made turns of up to 3 g's. Then he took the plane back down to 15,-000 feet where the low speed characteristics were evaluated with landing gear down. The flight ended with a straight-in approach and landing.

After this planned first flight, Oestricher commented, "It was a completely successful flight and a most enjoyable experience." He further said, "The airplane was very responsive to the controls at all times. Acceleration to maximum planned speed was accomplished very quickly. Another feature of the airplane that will impress all fighter pilots is the outstanding visibility through the single-piece canopy."

The second F-16 was delivered to Edwards AFB on February 27, 1974, again by a C-5 Galaxy. This second plane was painted in a camouflage pattern of sky blue and cloud white. This color pattern supposedly allowed the plane to blend in with the sky making it difficult for an enemy fighter or ground-based missile to spot, an important consideration for the air superiority mission that the lightweight fighter is designed to do. Besides being painted a different color, the second bird had a live gun in the mount along the fuselage just behind the pilot's seat. In the first F-16, there was only ballast. (The sky blue/white camouflage paint scheme would later be dropped as unsatisfactory and replaced by bluish-gray.)

The roll-out of the YF-16 was quite an occasion at General Dynamics-Forth Worth.

(General Dynamics Photo)

YF-16 FLIGHT TEST ACCOMPLISHMENTS

First Flight Prototype No. 1 . . . . 2 Feb 74

First Flight Prototype No. 2 . . . . 9 May 74

Total Flights to Date 330

Total Flight Hours to Date 417

Total Supersonic Hours to Date . . . . Nearly 14

Flights With No Discrepancies 169

Most Flights in One Day (YF-16 #1) 6

Quickest Turn Around Time Between Flights 11 Min 50 Sec

Greatest Number of Flights in One Month 47

Maximum Speed Attained . . . . Over Mach 2

Maximum Altitude Attained . . . . Over 60,000 Ft

Maximum "G" Attained 9

Longest Flight Without Refueling . . . . . . 2 Hrs 55 Min

Longest Flight With Refueling . . . . 4 Hrs 30 Min

Total Number of Air Refuelings 86

Total Number of Bombs Dropped . . . . 10 MK-84's

Total Rounds of Ammo Fired . . . . . . 12,948 Rounds

Total Number of Missiles Fired . . . . 7 AIM 9's

Number of Pilots to Fly YF-16 10

A number of details of the aft fuselage can be seen from this photo of the prototype during the fabrication process.   *(General Dynamics Photo)*

This photo clearly illustrates the prototype mating of the fuselage at Fort Worth.

(General Dynamics Photo)

Proof testing the flaperon of the prototype aircraft.   *(General Dynamics Photo)*

The F-16 being towed out for another test flight at Edwards AFB.   (Photo by Wil Andrepont)

YF-16 PROTOTYPE FLIGHT TEST PROGRAM

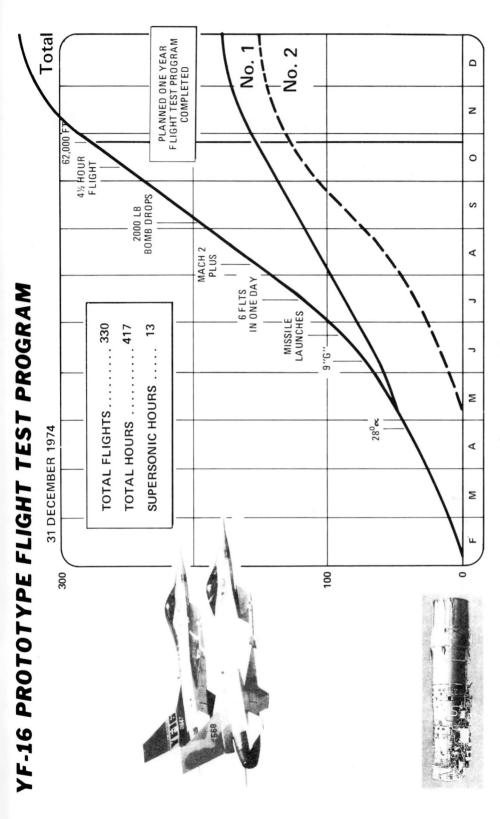

31 DECEMBER 1974

300

Total

62,000 FT

4½ HOUR FLIGHT

2000 LB BOMB DROPS

MACH 2 PLUS

6 FLTS IN ONE DAY

MISSILE LAUNCHES

9"G"

28°α

PLANNED ONE YEAR FLIGHT TEST PROGRAM COMPLETED

No. 1

No. 2

TOTAL FLIGHTS		330
TOTAL HOURS		417
SUPERSONIC HOURS		13

100

0

F M A M J J A S O N D

EXCELLENT AIR-TO-AIR AND AIR-TO-GROUND COMBAT CAPABILITIES HAVE BEEN DEMONSTRATED PROVIDING LOW-RISK ENTRY INTO FULL SCALE DEVELOPMENT AND PRODUCTION.

ENGINE HOURS (31 DECEMBER 1974)
Development & Ground Test . . . 27,900
Flight 8,025

Lifting its right wing gracefully, the YF-16 peels off into a dive.   (General Dynamics Photo)

YF-16 minus wings is placed aboard a giant C-5A Galaxy for trip to Edwards Air Force Base. *(General Dynamics Photo)*

Artist's concept of a pair of F-16's long before the first prototype flew. *(General Dynamics Photo)*

The final product ended up looking a lot like the early GD artist's concept.

(General Dynamics Photo)

Not exactly what you would call your standard operational paint job. The paint job adorned the aircraft that went to the Paris Air Show.

(USAF Photo)

The pilots who composed the Lightweight Fighter Test Force, and put the F-16 and F-17 through their paces in the fly-off, were both USAF and contractor test pilots. The Air Force pilots were from the Air Force Systems Command, the command responsible for developing new aircraft, and the Tactical Air Command, the command that will be the major user of the lightweight fighter. General Dynamics and Northrop pilots flew the F-16 and F-17, respectively. The flight test crews were broken up into three teams. One team flew F-16's and F-17's about an equal share of the time. Another team flew F-16's mostly, with a few flights in the F-17. The last team reversed this latter allocation of flying time. On basis of the evaluations and reports of these test pilots, the test force made its recommendation from a technical and performance standpoint as to which of the two craft the USAF should buy.

By the time each contractor submitted proposals for the full scale production program, the F-16's had reached the 300 flight milestone. This was in November 1974, just ten months after the first flight. During this time, the two F-16's had logged a total of 376 flying hours, of which more than 12 hours were at supersonic speeds. The craft had reached an altitude of more than 60,000 feet and a maximum speed of greater than Mach two. In over half the flights, the test pilots reported no flight discrepancies, an admirable achievement when testing an entirely new airplane. In these 300 flights, the pilots had put the two F-16's through just about every maneuver imaginable—high-energy climbs, turns, rolls, pull-ups, and push-overs.

During the flight test program, the aircraft's operational capability was assessed for both the air-to-air and air-to-ground missions. More than 11,000 rounds of 20mm ammunition were fired from the F-16's M-61 gun. The test pilots had target practice on towed targets and did ground strafing and participated in simulated air-to-ground missions. Some seven AIM-9, Sidewinder missiles were launched at both subsonic and supersonic speeds, and 2,000 pound bombs were dropped on targets.

The F-16, along with its competitor the F-17, was evaluated in the air combat role by pitting the craft against other current firstline U. S. fighter aircraft in simulated combat situations. These included F4E's from Tactical Air Command.

One of the two prototypes was painted in this unique light blue and grey camouflage paint scheme.   (General Dynamics Photo)

This shot shows the YF-16 in flight carrying two MK-83 bombs on wing pylons.
(General Dynamics Photo)

Besides evaluating the flight qualities, the maintenance aspects of the birds were not overlooked. This was an important consideration in picking one aircraft over the other because the Air Force wanted a plane with maximum operational utility and the lowest total lifetime cost—that is, the most economical one not only to produce, but to keep in the inventory for its full operational life. The F-16 was a very simple craft to maintain. During the flight test program it was amazing to see how few people and little ground support equipment it took to keep it flying. For example, on one day one F-16 was able to fly six times with full service between flights. These turn-arounds were as brief as 12 minutes from the time wheel chocks were placed under the wheels to the time the chocks were removed and the next sortie started.

But as is true with any test flight program, there was a glitch now and then to contend with. During a maximum weight takeoff demonstration in September 1974, the F-16 encountered an engine malfunction. A huge fireball was blown out of the nozzle and the engine continued to spew a plume of flame as the pilot brought the aircraft to a stop. Fortunately, neither the aircraft nor the engine sustained any serious damage.

On another occasion, General Dynamics' test pilot Neil Anderson was flying the number two bird over the GD facility at Fort Worth. While making his final approach he found that his right main landing gear would not drop down into position. He flew around Carswell AFB for about a half hour trying to correct the problem, with no success. Finally, he raised his left main and nose landing gear and made a nose high, gentle belly landing on the grass off to the side of the main runway. He skidded some 350 yards before stopping. Neil was unhurt and the damage to the F-16 was surprisingly light.

The pilots who flew the F-16's were very pleased with the airplane's flying characteristics, and the creature comforts it provided the driver. They readily adapted to the fly-by-wire control system and the force-sensing side-stick controller. They found that the fly-by-wire system gave the craft uniform handling characteristics under all altitude and Mach number conditions, that is the same effort was needed to be applied to the stick throughout the entire flight envelope. The increased comfort and higher g tolerance allowed by the 30-degree seatback angle also pleased the pilots as did the view from the clearview bubble canopy.

This paint scheme did not prove effective and was dropped early in the program.
(General Dynamics Photo)

F-16 shown being hoisted up after intentional wheels-up landing. Damage was light. Note left wing-tip
damage. *(General Dynamics Photo)*

The YF-16 pours it on going practically straight up!   *(USAF Photo)*

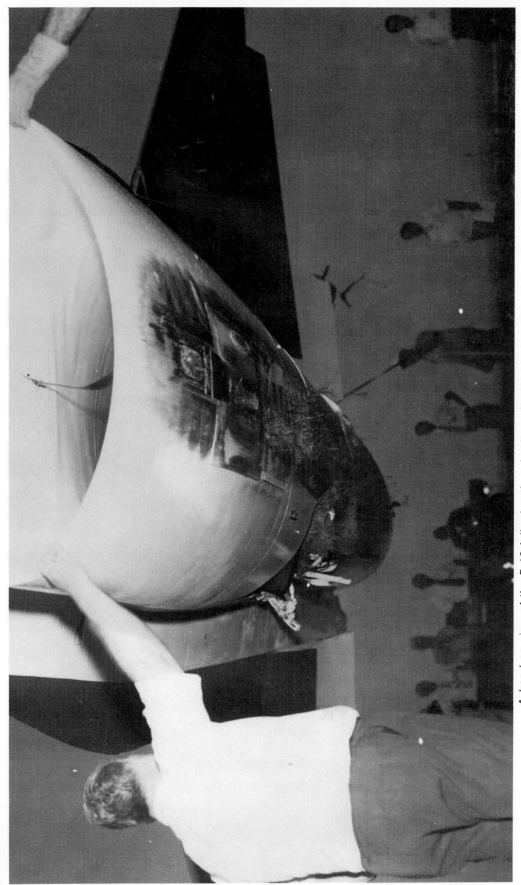

A head-on view of the F-16 following the wheels-up landing in the grass at Fort Worth. The aircraft picked up a little grass and dirt but the aircraft was quickly repaired. (General Dynamics Photo)

Then it was January 1975, and the flight testing of the F-16 and the competing F-17 had come to an end. It was time for General Dynamics to sit back and wait for the decision to go on. On January 13th, Secretary of the Air Force, John L. McLucas, made the announcement that the F-16 had been picked over the F-17 in the Air Combat Fighter Competition and the production of the F-16 would commence. In his announcement, he made the following comments about the fly-off flight test program:

"The flight test program that was conducted on the two lightweight fighters went extremely well. Both of the aircraft performed very well. Both of the contractors did an excellent job of supporting the prototype test program. Both of the engine companies did a good job of supporting the aircraft companies.

"On the other hand, there were significant differences in the performance of these prototypes. The YF-16 had many advantages in performance over the YF-17. It had advantages in agility, in acceleration, in turn rate and en-durance over the YF-17. These factors applied principally in the transonic and supersonic regimes. There were other advantages to the YF-16 over the YF-17. These factors included better tolerance of high G because of the tilt back seat, better visibility and better acceleration. In any case, the YF-16 met all the performance goals that we had established for it. The YF-17, while performing very well, did fall short of some of these goals. In the sub-sonic mission areas, the YF-16 and YF-17 were not as far apart as they were in the supersonic. This is indicative of the fact that the YF-16 had lower drag and was a cleaner design."

Mr. McLucas went on to say that flight test results were not the only factors that were considered in making the decision. There were the contractors' proposals for producing the aircraft and the overall system costs to also be considered. However, the flight test program provided the data needed to substantiate the contractor's claims and to indicate just how well the aircraft would do the Air Force's job once they got out into the field.

The standard grey camouflage paint scheme was later adapted for the YF-16.
(General Dynamics Photo)

Conventional bombs carried beneath wing of F-16.   *(Photo by Andrepont)*

Trio of bombs carried on a F-16 pylon.   *(Andrepont)*

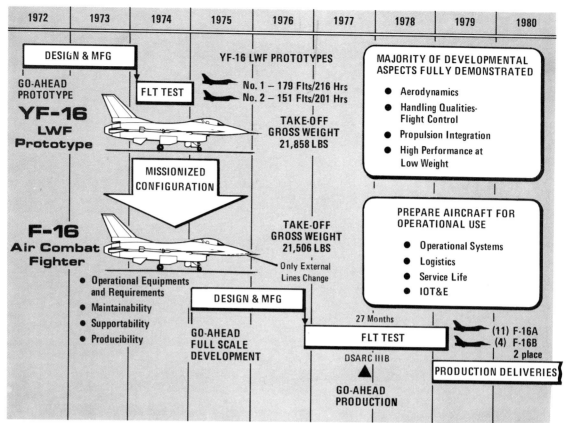

1972	1973	1974	1975	1976	1977	1978	1979	1980

DESIGN & MFG

GO-AHEAD
PROTOTYPE

YF-16
LWF
Prototype

FLT TEST

YF-16 LWF PROTOTYPES

No. 1 — 179 Flts/216 Hrs
No. 2 — 151 Flts/201 Hrs

**TAKE-OFF
GROSS WEIGHT
21,858 LBS**

**MAJORITY OF DEVELOPMENTAL
ASPECTS FULLY DEMONSTRATED**

- Aerodynamics
- Handling Qualities-
  Flight Control
- Propulsion Integration
- High Performance at
  Low Weight

**MISSIONIZED
CONFIGURATION**

F-16
Air Combat
Fighter

- Operational Equipments
  and Requirements
- Maintainability
- Supportability
- Producibility

**TAKE-OFF
GROSS WEIGHT
21,506 LBS**

Only External
Lines Change

**PREPARE AIRCRAFT FOR
OPERATIONAL USE**

- Operational Systems
- Logistics
- Service Life
- IOT&E

DESIGN & MFG

GO-AHEAD
FULL SCALE
DEVELOPMENT

27 Months

FLT TEST

DSARC IIIB

GO-AHEAD
PRODUCTION

(11) F-16A
(4) F-16B
2 place

PRODUCTION DELIVERIES

F-16 development and production schedule.   *(General Dynamics Photo)*

*A number of tests were performed on somewhat differently configured F-16 models. A model is shown
here mounted in an Arnold Engineering Development Center (AEDC) Wind Tunnel.   (USAF Photo)*

This particular F-16 wind tunnel model features forward canard surfaces mounted on the base of the engine intake. *(USAF Photo)*

The F-16's blended flowing lines are clearly illustrated by this AEDC Wind Tunnel Model. *(USAF Photo)*

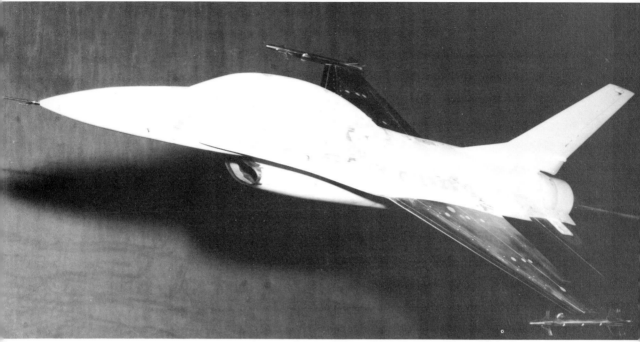

A wind tunnel model of the 2-seater F-16B is tested in an AEDC Wind Tunnel.   *(USAF Photo)*

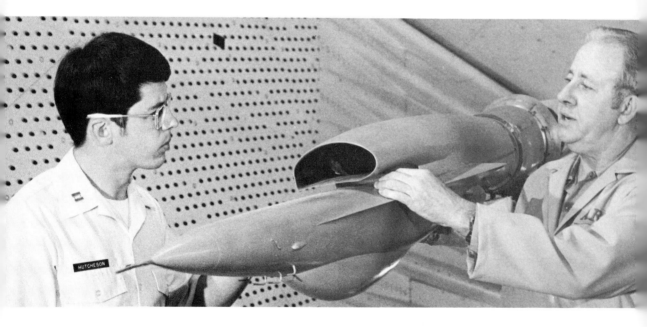

Inlet performance characteristics of the Air Force's new Air Combat Fighter, the General Dynamics F-16, were mapped in a series of wind tunnel tests at Systems Command's Arnold Engineering Development Center. Both the transonic and supersonic 16-foot tunnels were used in studying the inlet throughout the aircraft's complete speed/maneuvering envelope. In the transonic tests the .15-scale model was tested at angles of attack from minus 10 degrees to 35 degrees, while in supersonic speeds data were taken at angles of attack up to 20 degrees. Two forebody models were used in the tests—a standard production configuration and one fitted with nose strakes. At lower flight speeds, airflow through the engine intake was generated by the tunnel's scavenging scoop (normally used to remove combustion gases in engine testing) through a connection developed by personnel at ARO, Inc., the center's operating contractor. Shown with the model in the transonic wind tunnel are Capt. Charles M. Hutcheson, an Air Force test director in the Propulsion Wind Tunnel facility, and Ernie DuBose, a test facility craftsman for ARO, Inc.
(USAF-AEDC Photo)

HiMAT

SPEED	SUPERSONIC
MANEUVERING	8G PERFORMANCE
LAUNCH WEIGHT	3400 LB
ENGINE	GENERAL ELECTRIC J85-21

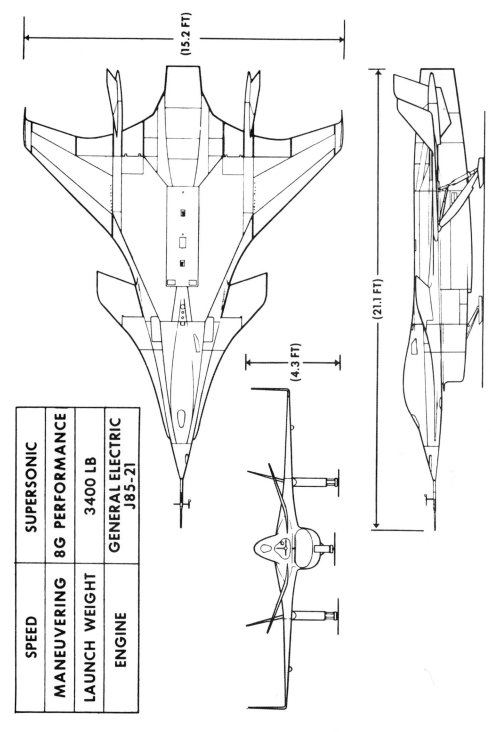

(15.2 FT)

(4.3 FT)

(21.1 FT)

The HiMAT, a NASA research aircraft for testing advanced military and civilian aviation needs of the 1980's, bears an amazing resemblance to the F-16.
(NASA Drawing)

View of the F-16 test aircraft being modified at General Dynamics to the Controlled Configured Vehicle configuration.   (General Dynamics Photo)

The only external CCV modification is the addition of canard surfaces placed under the YF-16's inlet—one on each side of the nose wheel. Changes to the all-electrical flight control system, together with use of the canards and normal control surfaces, provide direct lift and direct sideforce control. Direct lift is produced by the combined motion of the horizontal stabilator and wing flaperons. Direct sideforce results from coordinated deflection of the canards and the rudder. Use of these additional control freedoms will allow new means for controlling the aircraft and will provide better target tracking performance and weapon delivery accuracy.

Traditionally, aircraft are designed to return to straight and level flight in a "hands-off" condition, calling for large wing and tail surfaces. The greater the built-in stability, the larger the control surfaces needed to maneuver the aircraft. In a control configured vehicle, onboard instrumentation constantly monitors flight conditions and adjusts control surfaces to insure stability. This permits the use of smaller wings, tail surfaces and control surfaces, with the resultant saving in drag and weight.

The fuel system was also modified to provide a means for in-flight control of the aircraft's center-of-gravity. This feature allows testing of the aircraft at different levels of aerodynamic stability. While positive stability is needed for the pilot to control the airplane, the CCV airplane obtains the required stability through the control system in place of built-in aerodynamic stability. The result is decreased air resistance on the airplane in flight and improved maneuvering capability.

If the tests prove successful on the YF-16, we can expect to see future fighters that may not only look different but include radically different performance characteristics.

(General Dynamics Photo)

Chapter IV
The Other Faces of the F-16

The F-16 production program could possibly become the biggest aircraft program in aviation history. The United States Air Force is planning on initially buying 650 of the craft including a two-seater trainer version designated the F-16B. The total number of F-16's supplied to the USAF could reach over 1400 within the next decade.

In order to get the additional seat in the F-16B, the F-16 fuselage has to be stretched about 10 inches. The additional section is added just aft of the normal cockpit. Also a new and longer bubble canopy has to be used. Both of the seats in the F-16B have the 30-degree rearward tilt found so successful in the test program.

Besides filling USAF needs, the F-16 will be finding its way into air forces throughout the world. The first countries which are planning to use the F-16 are four members of a European consortium who evaluated various aircraft manufacturers' designs for possible replacements for their aging Lockheed F-104's. The four members of this consortium are Belgium, The

Netherlands, Denmark, and Norway.

In gaining the approval of this consortium, the F-16 has had some strong competition from some fine European-developed fighters in the lightweight class, and again its American competitor, the F-17. There was the Mirage F1E developed by Dassault-Breguet of France, and from SAAB-Scania of Sweden came the Viggen 37E.

While the European contenders and the F-17 are all fine airplanes, the F-16 had a lot of good things going for it. F-16 incorporated the latest in technology, while the Mirage and SAAB aircraft were relatively old designs. The F1E was first flown in December 1966, while the Viggen made its maiden flight only a couple of months later. Although both planes had updated components such as avionics and engines, the basic designs remained the same. They did not have such advances in technology as fly-by-wire, side-stick control, carbon composite components, and the newer engine technology that was found in the F-16.

F-16 competitor, the Mirage F1E in flight.   (Dassault Photo)

The losing French competitor—the Mirage F1E—parked at the Paris Air Show.   *(USAF Photo)*

Details of the Mirage F1E are shown as it appeared at 1975 Paris Air Show.   *(USAF Photo)*

The interesting camouflage technique of the Viggen is shown by this photo.   (SAAB Photo)

A beautiful flight of SAAB Viggens in formation. *(SAAB Photo)*

Between it and the two European designs, the F-16 provided better performance in every category except for perhaps maximum speed. The Mirage could travel at speeds up to Mach 2.2 to 2.5 versus the Mach 2 limit of the SAAB, the F-17 and the F-16. The F-16 could carry a greater load, had a greater radius of action, and was more maneuverable since it could sustain higher g's than the Europeans. In addition, the F-16 had the lowest fuel cost per flying hour, a vital consideration for fuel-short Europe, and the maintenance costs per flying hour were expected to be the lowest for the F-16.

All in all, the F-16 turned out to be the best choice for the consortium, even though many Europeans argued that a European fighter should be of European design. The fact that the United States was going to purchase substantial quantities of the F-16

played no small part in the consortium's decision. First, the large production volume meant a lower cost per plane since the research and development costs and special tooling costs could be spread, or amortized, over a larger number of planes. Secondly, since the USAF's F-16's will be flying alongside the consortium's planes in NATO support, there will be a standard plane used throughout NATO, a goal the Europeans have been striving for to reduce logistics and maintenance problems.

The F-16's purchased by the consortium, however, will be partly built and tested in the consortium member's own territories. Part of the deal between the American airplane and engine contractors is to minimize the actual flow of money from the consortium countries to the United States in payment for the craft. This is accomplished by fabricating and

The Viggen is a highly versatile aircraft. This photo shows its deployment from a normal road.

(SAAB Photo)

assembling part of the European F-16's in Europe, and by paying for the remainder of the cost in part by making parts and sub-assemblies for USAF planes in lieu of paying cash. This is termed "offsetting" the costs. For example, two Belgian firms, Fairey and SABCA, will supply aircraft for the Belgian and Royal Danish Air Forces. The aft fuselage, along with the vertical finbox, will be manufactured by Fairey who will also mate the airframe sections. SABCA will build the wing box and will be responsible for final aircraft assembly and actual delivery to the users. Fokker-VFW in The Netherlands will fabricate the leading edge flaps, the trailing edge flaperons, and the center fuselage. The Dutch firm will also handle mating, final assembly, and delivery to the Dutch and Norwegian Air Forces. There are also plans for the Europeans to participate in building the F100 engine, and other parts of the planes that include such items as navigation and electronics equipment, radar antennas, landing gear, and computers. On the other side of the coin, the three European manufacturers would produce some 2,800 pounds of the F-16 ship's total 6,500 pounds of airframe components. In all, about forty percent of the value of each European plane would be produced in Europe and for USAF F-16's, about ten percent would be of European origin. To further increase the offsetting of costs, the Europeans may be producing items that have only indirect effect on the F-16. For example, they may make parts for other General Dynamics or Pratt and Whitney products. They may also produce such items as shipping containers, paper, and office supplies for use by the F-16 program. Currently, it is estimated that over eighty percent of the aircraft cost can be offset by overseas production.

The three European manufacturing firms will be supplying parts that will be used in development aircraft still to be built. Engineers from overseas will participate in F-16 development at General Dynamics' Fort Worth facility.

The Europeans also want some modifications to their F-16 to meet their own requirements. Norway and Denmark want to be able to fire the McDonnell Douglas Harpoon anti-ship missile. All four countries do not desire the air-refueling capability. Norway wants a braking parachute to assist in landing on the icy runways so common in that part of the world. Other changes would include modified auto-pilots, and addition of such items as a radar altimeter, windshield anti-icing equipment, and a video tape recorder.

F-16 deliveries to Europe will begin in 1979, the same year the USAF will start to get the craft. Belgium wants 116 F-16's, 102 will go to The Netherlands, 73 will carry the Norwegian flag, while the Danish Air Force will get 59, for a total buy of 350. Both the United States and General Dynamics hope these initial commitments are just the "tip of the iceberg," and that more planes can be sold to the consortium and to other countries. Estimates for as many as 2000 to 3000 craft have been forecasted by several experts.

The F-16 did not fare as well in the competition to meet U. S. Navy requirements, however. The Navy's lightweight fighter program originally carried the acronym VFAX, but this title was later changed to a more descriptive one, Navy Air Combat Fighter, NACF for short. The Navy wanted a replacement for the McDonnell Douglas F-4 and the Ling-Temco-Vought A-7 that was both affordable and effective. The NACF would accomplish some F-4 missions and eventually replace the A-7 and possibly other special mission aircraft. The NACF would complement the

An aerial view of the giant General Dynamics-Fort Worth plant. This plant, over its 32-year history, has produced over 4,000 strategic and tactical military aircraft. It is the production site for the F-16. (General Dynamics Photo)

A view inside the Fort Worth G.D. facility with one of the F-16 prototypes. (USAF Photo)

87

F-16 PRODUCTION -- A NATIONAL PROGRAM

DISTRIBUTION OF OUTSIDE PROCUREMENT

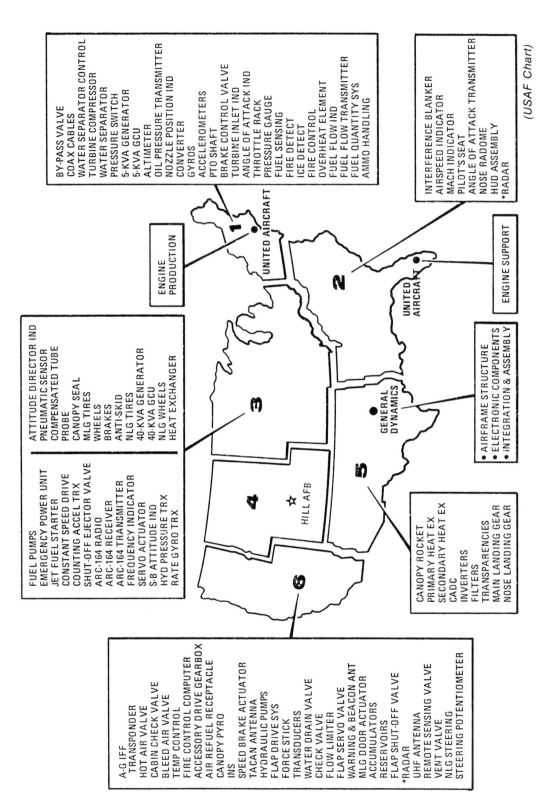

UNITED AIRCRAFT (1)
- BY-PASS VALVE
- COAX CABLES
- WATER SEPARATOR CONTROL
- TURBINE COMPRESSOR
- WATER SEPARATOR
- PRESSURE SWITCH
- 5-KVA GENERATOR
- 5-KVA GCU
- ALTIMETER
- OIL PRESSURE TRANSMITTER
- NOZZLE POSITION IND
- CONVERTER
- GYROS
- ACCELEROMETERS
- PTO SHAFT
- BRAKE CONTROL VALVE
- TURBINE INLET IND
- ANGLE OF ATTACK IND
- THROTTLE RACK
- PRESSURE GAUGE
- FUEL SENSING
- FIRE DETECT
- ICE DETECT
- FIRE CONTROL
- OVERHEAT ELEMENT
- FUEL FLOW IND
- FUEL FLOW TRANSMITTER
- FUEL QUANTITY SYS
- AMMO HANDLING

UNITED AIRCRAFT (2)
- INTERFERENCE BLANKER
- AIRSPEED INDICATOR
- MACH INDICATOR
- PILOT'S SEAT
- ANGLE OF ATTACK TRANSMITTER
- NOSE RADOME
- HUD ASSEMBLY
- *RADAR

ENGINE PRODUCTION

ENGINE SUPPORT

(3)
- ATTITUDE DIRECTOR IND
- PNEUMATIC SENSOR
- COMPENSATED TUBE
- PROBE
- CANOPY SEAL
- MLG TIRES
- WHEELS
- BRAKES
- ANTI-SKID
- NLG TIRES
- 40-KVA GENERATOR
- 40-KVA GCU
- NLG WHEELS
- HEAT EXCHANGER

(4)
- FUEL PUMPS
- EMERGENCY POWER UNIT
- JET FUEL STARTER
- CONSTANT SPEED DRIVE
- COUNTING ACCEL TRX
- SHUT-OFF EJECTOR VALVE
- ARC-164 RADIO
- ARC-164 RECEIVER
- ARC-164 TRANSMITTER
- FREQUENCY INDICATOR
- SERVO ACTUATOR
- S-B ATTITUDE IND
- HYD PRESSURE TRX
- RATE GYRO TRX

HILL AFB

(5) GENERAL DYNAMICS
- AIRFRAME STRUCTURE
- ELECTRONIC COMPONENTS
- INTEGRATION & ASSEMBLY

(5)
- CANOPY ROCKET
- PRIMARY HEAT EX
- SECONDARY HEAT EX
- CADC
- INVERTERS
- FILTERS
- TRANSPARENCIES
- MAIN LANDING GEAR
- NOSE LANDING GEAR

(6)
- A-G IFF
- TRANSPONDER
- HOT AIR VALVE
- CABIN CHECK VALVE
- BLEED AIR VALVE
- TEMP CONTROL
- FIRE CONTROL COMPUTER
- ACCESSORY DRIVE GEARBOX
- AIR REFUEL RECEPTACLE
- CANOPY PYRO
- INS
- SPEED BRAKE ACTUATOR
- TACAN ANTENNA
- HYDRAULIC PUMPS
- FLAP DRIVE SYS
- FORCE STICK
- TRANSDUCERS
- WATER DRAIN VALVE
- CHECK VALVE
- FLOW LIMITER
- FLAP SERVO VALVE
- WARNING & BEACON ANT
- MLG DOOR ACTUATOR
- ACCUMULATORS
- RESERVOIRS
- FLAP SHUT-OFF VALVE
- *RADAR
- UHF ANTENNA
- REMOTE SENSING VALVE
- VENT VALVE
- NLG STEERING
- STEERING POTENTIOMETER

(USAF Chart)

Production and cost considerations

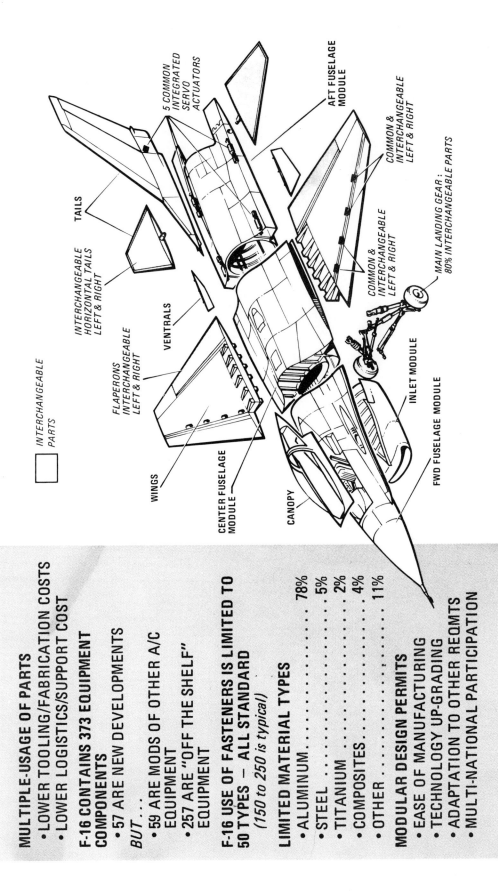

5 COMMON INTEGRATED SERVO ACTUATORS

TAILS

INTERCHANGEABLE HORIZONTAL TAILS LEFT & RIGHT

FLAPERONS INTERCHANGEABLE LEFT & RIGHT

VENTRALS

WINGS

CENTER FUSELAGE MODULE

CANOPY

AFT FUSELAGE MODULE

COMMON & INTERCHANGEABLE LEFT & RIGHT

COMMON & INTERCHANGEABLE LEFT & RIGHT

MAIN LANDING GEAR: 80% INTERCHANGEABLE PARTS

INLET MODULE

FWD FUSELAGE MODULE

INTERCHANGEABLE PARTS

(General Dynamics Drawing)

MULTIPLE-USAGE OF PARTS
- LOWER TOOLING/FABRICATION COSTS
- LOWER LOGISTICS/SUPPORT COST

F-16 CONTAINS 373 EQUIPMENT COMPONENTS
- 57 ARE NEW DEVELOPMENTS

BUT . . .
- 59 ARE MODS OF OTHER A/C EQUIPMENT
- 257 ARE "OFF THE SHELF" EQUIPMENT

F-16 USE OF FASTENERS IS LIMITED TO 50 TYPES — ALL STANDARD
(150 to 250 is typical)

LIMITED MATERIAL TYPES
- ALUMINUM 78%
- STEEL 5%
- TITANIUM 2%
- COMPOSITES 4%
- OTHER 11%

MODULAR DESIGN PERMITS
- EASE OF MANUFACTURING
- TECHNOLOGY UP-GRADING
- ADAPTATION TO OTHER REQMTS
- MULTI-NATIONAL PARTICIPATION

89

(USAF Photo)

Views of the winning F-16 taking its bows at the Paris Air Show.   *(USAF Photo)*

The F-16 rolls toward takeoff position at the 1975 Paris Air Show. The details of the blended fuselage are readily apparent. *(USAF Photo)*

Grumman F-14 with the F-14 performing the more demanding and sophisticated missions and the NACF used for the "bread and butter" fighter escort and visual attack missions.

The Navy looked at a wide range of proposals for the NACF assignment including the F-16 and F-17, or versions thereof. There was a McDonnell Douglas concept that incorporated canards above the engine intakes, two vertical takeoff and landing (VTOL) ideas, one each from Rockwell International and General Dynamics. Another alternative considered by the Navy was a stripped-down version of the Grumman swing-wing F-14 Tomcat. It was thought a lightweight F-14, without the costly electronics package and the Phoenix missile, would make a hot Navy combat lightweight fighter.

For the NACF competition, the F-16 and F-17 contractors teamed up with other contractors who had more experience with carrier-based aircraft. General Dynamics teamed up with Ling-Temco-Vought and Northrop paired up with McDonnell Douglas. The version of the F-16 derived for Navy and Marine flyers was considerably different than its USAF brother. Designated the Model 1601, the seagoing version of the F-16 would have a stretched fuselage and an uprated powerplant. The 1601 bird would also have its wing area increased by some fifty-seven square feet.

But this was one competition the F-16 was not able to win. The Navy picked a version of the F-17 for its lightweight fighter. The F-17 was modified to such an extent for the Navy job that it was given a new designation, the F-18.

91

Artist's concept of Rockwell International's VTOL, proposed craft for the Navy's lightweight fighter competition. The craft is currently being constructed in a two prototype development program for the Navy. *(Rockwell-International Photo)*

An artist's concept of a VTOL aircraft studied by General Dynamics. Aircraft had no relationship to Fort Worth based F-16 program. *(General Dynamics Photo)*

The VTOL characteristics of the General Dynamics concept are shown by this drawing.
(General Dynamics Photo)

An F-14 going through its paces at the 1975 Paris Air Show.   (USAF Photo)

A stripped-out version of the F-14 Tomcat was also taken into consideration in the Navy's competition.   (U. S. Navy Photo)

An artist's concept of the Navy F-16 which, as of this writing, will never be. (LTV Aerospace Photo)

The F-18—the Navy counterpart to the USAF F-16.   (McDonnell-Douglas Photo)

F-18 NAVY AIR COMBAT FIGHTER

Cutaway view of the F-18 Navy Air Combat Fighter.

(McDonnell-Douglas Drawing)

MCDONNELL DOUGLAS

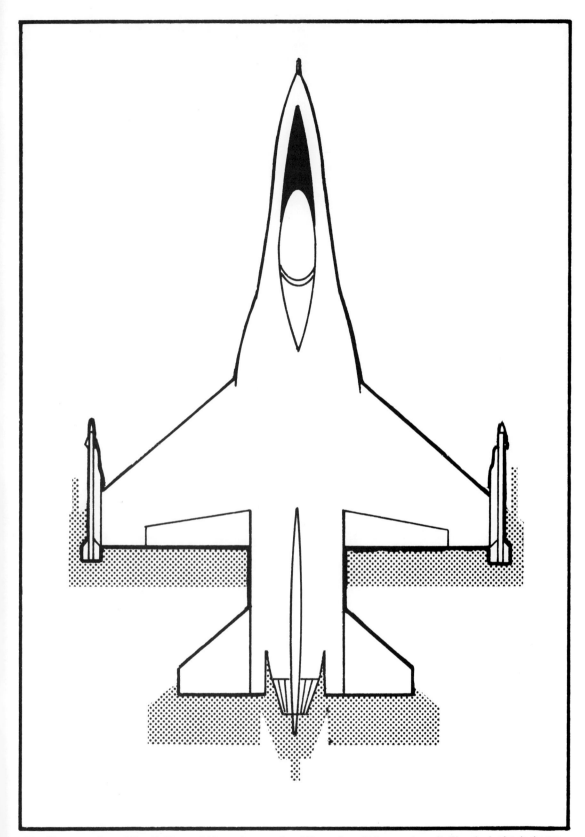

The Navy version of the F-16 would have been a far different and bigger aircraft. The dark shaded area shows the postulated Navy version. *(Artwork by Frank Stallman)*

Flying mate of the F-16 during the late 1970's and 1980's will be the F-15 Eagle. (USAF Photo)

Chapter V
What It All Means

The F-16 program will mean jobs for some 55,000 to 65,000 people who will work for several hundred suppliers and sub-contractors throughout the country. During the development phase of the program about 4,000 new jobs will be created at General Dynamics Fort Worth and the number of new jobs here will grow to about 7,000 during the peak production period. The European production will create up to about 6,000 additional jobs during the early 1980's. Indeed, this super-size program will have a major impact on the economy of the aerospace industry for years to come.

The F-16/F-17 prototyping approach has shown the merits of the "fly-before-buy" concept. The next aircraft whose selection will be made by this method is the military's Advanced Medium STOL Transport (AMST). STOL stands for Short Takeoff and Landing. The contest here is between Boeing's YC-14 and the McDonnell Douglas YC-15. The outcome of this decision will not only have a bearing on the future military transport fleet, but on civilian transports as well.

The USAF combat fighter force of the 1980's will be composed of a mixture of F-15's and F-16's. These craft not only offer superior performance, but do so for reduced operations and maintenance costs.

Lt. General James Stewart, the commander of the USAF's Aeronautical Systems Division (manager for the development of the Air Force's new airplanes including the F-16) has made some comments about the capability of the F-16 in comparison with its potential adversaries in combat, the Soviet Union's fleet of firstline fighters and bombers. The F-16 will have greater maneuverability and better acceleration than the MiG-21. This will allow the F-16 pilot to maintain the initiative in both starting and stopping air engagements. The F-16 will have a far greater combat radius, be twice as effective in air-to-ground combat, and generally be more agile than the MiG-21. The MiG-21 does have a greater supersonic dash speed, its only advantage over the F-16.

The F-16 will also be superior to the MiG-23, except for top speed, according to General Stewart. In comparison to the MiG-25, the F-16 could outperform this high-altitude Mach 3.0 craft up to a speed of about Mach 1.6, then the MiG-25 could run away from the F-16. However, the F-16 could intercept the MiG-25 with the assistance of an advanced ground-based intercept radar. The F 16 would also be very effective against the Soviet Mach 2 class bombers, especially at the lower altitudes.

All in all, the F-16 is a real flying machine and USAF pilots both young and old are itching to get behind the stick of one.

The YF-16 above the desert at Edwards AFB.   *(General Dynamics Photo)*

The MiG 21 Fishbed is a first-line Soviet fighter aircraft.

The MiG 21 is a fighter which has been modified many times.
Many satellite countries are equipped with this aircraft.

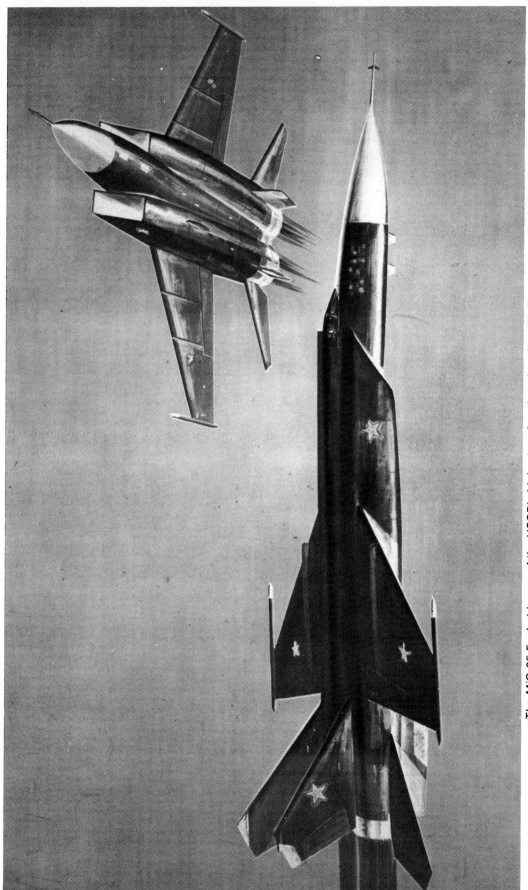

The MiG 25 Foxbat is one of the USSR's highest performing aircraft.   (McDonnell-Douglas Photo)

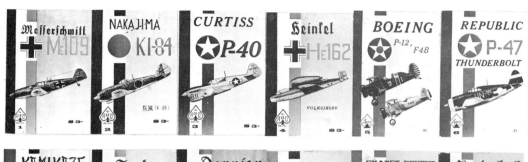

AERO SERIES

A detailed look at many of the world's most famous and noteworthy military aircraft. Each book contains historical commentary, selected photographic material covering all aspects of the aircraft, technical data and specifications, four pages of color drawings, plus much more. Provides an unprecedented source of material for the modeler, military enthusiast, collector and historian.

Volumes 1 thru 20 $3.00(A) each.

ISBN 0-8168-0500-8	Vol. 1	MESSERSCHMITT ME 109		ISBN 0-8168-0540-7	Vol. 11	CHANCE VOUGHT F4U "Corsair"
ISBN 0-8168-0504-0	Vol. 2	NAKAJIMA KI-84		ISBN 0-8168-0544-X	Vol. 12	HEINKEL 100, 112
ISBN 0-8168-0508-3	Vol. 3	CURTISS P-40		ISBN 0-8168-0548-2	Vol. 13	HEINKEL 177 "Greif"
ISBN 0-8168-0512-1	Vol. 4	HEINKEL HE 162		ISBN 0-8168-0552-0	Vol. 14	MESSERSCHMITT 262
ISBN 0-8168-0516-4	Vol. 5	BOEING P-12, F4B		ISBN 0-8168-0556-3	Vol. 15	NORTH AMERICAN P-51 "Mustang"
ISBN 0-8168-0520-2	Vol. 6	REPUBLIC P-47		ISBN 0-8168-0560-1	Vol. 16	MESSERSCHMITT Bf 110
ISBN 0-8168-0524-5	Vol. 7	KAMIKAZE		ISBN 0-8168-0564-4	Vol. 17	MESSERSCHMITT 163 "Komet"
ISBN 0-8168-0528-8	Vol. 8	JUNKERS Ju 87 "Stuka"		ISBN 0-8168-0568-7	Vol. 18	FOCKE-WULF 190 "Wurger"
ISBN 0-8168-0532-6	Vol. 9	DORNIER Do-335 "Pfeil"		ISBN 0-8168-0572-5	Vol. 19	LOCKHEED P-38 "Lightning"
ISBN 0-8168-0536-9	Vol. 10	SUPERMARINE SPITFIRE		ISBN 0-8168-0576-8	Vol. 20	GRUMMAN F8F "Bearcat"

NEW ENLARGED 104-page SERIES ➡

ISBN 0-8168-0580-6	Vol. 21	GRUMMAN TBF/TBM "Avenger"	$3.95(A)
ISBN 0-8168-0582-2	Vol. 21	GRUMMAN TBF/TBM SUPPLEMENT	$1.95(A)
ISBN 0-8168-0584-9	Vol. 22	BOEING P-26 "Peashooter"	$3.95(A)
ISBN 0-8168-0586-5	Vol. 23	DOUGLAS TBD-1 "Devastator"	$3.95(A)
ISBN 0-8168-0588-1	Vol. 24	BOEING B-52 "Stratofortress"	$6.95(A)
ISBN 0-8168-0592-X	Vol. 25	GRUMMAN F-14 "Tomcat"	$6.95(A)
ISBN 0-8168-0596-2	Vol. 26	GENERAL DYNAMICS F-16	$6.95(A)